Kentucky

By Kimberly Valzania

Consultant
Nanci R. Vargus, Ed.D.
Primary Multiage Teacher
Decatur Township Schools, Indianapolis, Indiana

Children's Press®
A Division of Scholastic Inc.
New York   Toronto   London   Auckland   Sydney
Mexico City   New Delhi   Hong Kong
Danbury, Connecticut

Designer: Herman Adler Design
Photo Researcher: Caroline Anderson
The photo on the cover shows Kentucky Horse State Park.

Library of Congress Cataloging-in-Publication Data

Valzania, Kim.
  Kentucky / by Kimberly Valzania.
      p. cm. – (Rookie read-about geography)
Includes index.
Summary: A simple introduction to Kentucky, focusing on its regions and their geographical features.
  ISBN 0-516-22697-5 (lib. bdg.)   0-516-27842-8 (pbk.)
  1. Kentucky–Juvenile literature. 2. Kentucky–Geography–Juvenile literature. [1. Kentucky.] I. Title. II. Series.
  F451.3 .V35 2003
  917.69–dc21   2002011533

JE
VAL
C. 1

$14.25

1 2 3 4 5 6 7 8 9 10 R 12 11 10 09 08 07 06 05 04 03

Where is the longest cave in the world?

In the state of Kentucky!

Kentucky is west of
the Virginias and east of
Missouri. The Ohio River
borders Kentucky to the
north. Tennessee is its
neighbor to the south.

CANADA

WASHINGTON

OREGON

IDAHO

MONTANA

WYOMING

NEVADA

UTAH

CALIFORNIA

ARIZONA

NEW MEXICO

NORTH
DAKOTA

SOUTH
DAKOTA

NEBRASKA

COLORADO

KANSAS

OKLAHOMA

TEXAS

MINNESOTA

WISCONSIN

IOWA

ILLINOIS

MISSOURI

ARKANSAS

LOUISIANA

MICHIGAN

INDIANA

OHIO

KENTUCKY

TENNESSEE

MISSISSIPPI

ALABAMA

GEORGIA

FLORIDA

NEW HAMPSHIRE

VERMONT

MAINE

NEW YORK

PENNSYLVANIA

WEST
VIRGINIA

VIRGINIA

NORTH
CAROLINA

SOUTH
CAROLINA

MASSACHUSETTS

RHODE ISLAND

CONNECTICUT

NEW JERSEY

DELAWARE

MARYLAND

Washington, D.C.

ALASKA

CANADA

MEXICO

HAWAII

North

West   East

South

The climate (KLYE-mit) in Kentucky is mild. Weather that stays the same most of the time is called climate.

It snows a little in the winter, but mostly in the mountains. The summers are very hot.

Many different kinds of
animals live in Kentucky.
You can see deer and wild
turkeys in the woods.

The rivers and streams have fish and otters. Some of the caves are filled with bats.

In the center of Kentucky there are grassy plains.

This part of Kentucky is called the Bluegrass region (REE-juhn). You can find racehorses here.

The grass in the Bluegrass region looks a little blue.

The soil is good for farming. Soybeans and tobacco grow there.

13

14

The southern (SUHTH-urn) edge of the Bluegrass region is called the Knobs (NOBZ). It is named for the hundreds of cone-shaped hills there. The hills are made of sandstone.

Frankfort and Louisville are two major cities in the Bluegrass region. Frankfort is the state capital. Louisville is the largest city.

Louisville

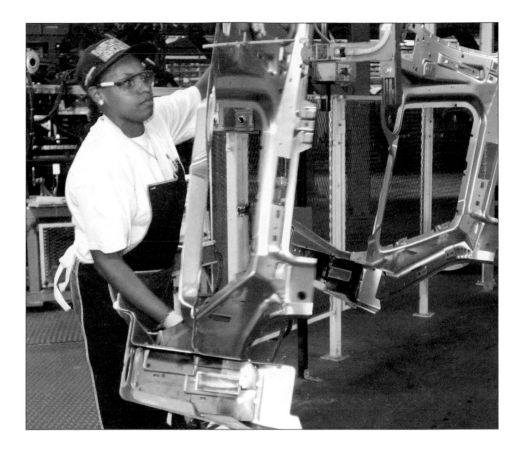

Many people who live in these cities work in hospitals, factories, and schools.

The Appalachian (a-puh-LAY-shee-uhn) Mountains are in the eastern part of Kentucky. This region is called the Appalachian Plateau (pla-TOH).

Black Mountain is here. It is Kentucky's highest point.

In this part of Kentucky you will find many talented people. They play instruments such as the dulcimer (DUHL-suh-muhr).

They also weave and
make furniture.

Another region in Kentucky
is the Western Coal Field.
Can you find it on the map?

Many of the people who live
here are coal miners.

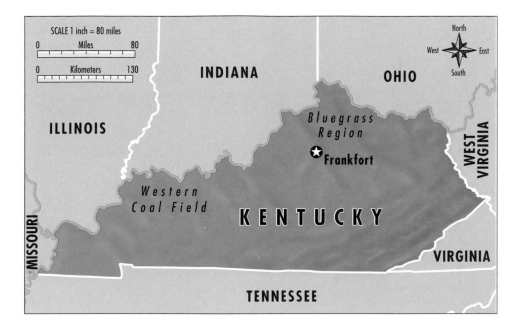

SCALE 1 inch = 80 miles

0   Miles   80

0   Kilometers   130

North

West   East

South

INDIANA

OHIO

ILLINOIS

Bluegrass Region

⭐ Frankfort

Western Coal Field

WEST VIRGINIA

K E N T U C K Y

MISSOURI

VIRGINIA

TENNESSEE

23

24

The Pennyroyal Region is in the south. Many streams run under the ground there. They wash away the limestone and form caves.

The longest cave in the world is in the Pennyroyal Region. It is called Mammoth Cave and is more than 300 miles long!

Many visitors come to Mammoth Cave every year.

If you were a visitor
to Kentucky, which part
would you like to see first?

Words You Know

Appalachian Mountains

dulcimer

Louisville

30

Mammoth Cave

the Knobs

racehorses

soybeans

Index

About the Author

Kimberly Valzania lives in Connecticut with her husband and two young children. She has worked as a freelance writer of educational books and other materials for the past five years.

Photo Credits

Photographs © 2003: Buddy Mays/Travel Stock: 20, 30 bottom left; Corbis Images: 7 bottom (Kevin R. Morris), 24 (David Muench), 17 (Reuters NewMedia Inc.); Dan Dry & Assoc.: 10 bottom, 21, 28, 31 bottom left; Dembinsky Photo Assoc.: 8 (Mike Barlow), 3, 10 top (Dan Dempster), 16, 30 bottom right (Mark E. Gibson), 7 top (Michael P. Hubrich), 9 (Philip Perry); H. Armstrong Roberts, Inc./Roy E. Roper: 13 top, 31 bottom right; Kentucky Dept of Travel: 27, 31 top left; Kentucky Geological Survey/Richard Smath: 14, 31 top right; Photo Researchers, NY/Adam Jones: 19, 30 top; The Image Works/David Frazier: 13 bottom; Tom Till Photography, Inc.: cover.

Maps by Bob Italiano